Yes,

you can learn
KOREAN language structure
in 40 minutes!

Tongku Lee

HOLLYM

Elizabeth,NJ • Seoul

Yes, you can learn Korean language structure in 40 Minutes !

Wow !!
You will be able to read and
write Korean after
investing 40 minutes
in this book!!
*You'd better
believe it !!!*

Yes, you can learn
Korean language structure in 40 minutes !

Copyright © 1998, 1999, 2004
by Tongku Lee

First published in 1998
Second revised edition, 1999
Third revised edition, 2004
Second printing, 2005
by Hollym International Corp.
18 Donald Place, Elizabeth, New Jersey 07208, USA
Phone (908)353-1655   Fax (908)353-0255
http://www.hollym.com

Published simultaneously in Korea
by Hollym Corporation; Publishers
13-13 Gwancheol-dong, Jongno-gu, Seoul 110-111, Korea
Phone (02)735-7551~4   Fax (02)730-5149, 8192
http://www.hollym.co.kr E-mail: info@hollym.co.kr

ISBN : 1-56591-091-5

Printed in Korea

A CORDIAL INVITATION

- The primary goal of this book is to provide the reader with the fundamentals for the structural understanding of written Korean.

- The author's unique methodology will guide you through the process, making your learning experience fun and interesting: you, too, will soon find yourself enjoying learning the basics of Korean language structure.

GOOD LUCK !!!

AUTHOR'S INTRODUCTION

Adequately, and in accordance with my wishes, a script of mine metamorphosed into the first edition of this book in 1998. The methodology I have developed assumes a hypothetical connection between a given culture and its language. I would henceforth appreciate any input or suggestions that might improve the overall quality of this learning tool. And I cordially wish you the best of luck in your Korean learning experience.

I'd like to thank my wife and son who both contributed to this book in earnest.

Tongku Lee
Seoul, Korea
March 2004

PREFACE

- Of the layout: with a great deal of diagrams and illustrations in this book, skimming readers may easily acquire the basic idea of this book just by skimming through the pages.

- Of making the title: after numerous trials on introducing this methodology to a group of non-experienced learners of Korean it took an average of 40 minutes to teach. That is how this title came about.

- For variation in pronunciation, and to avoid possible mishaps, all Korean-English correspondences have been in accordance with the US standard. Furthermore, inscriptions of phonetic values have been omitted for the sake of simplicity.

A FASCINATING APPROACH TO THE LEARNING OF KOREAN LANGUAGE STRUCTURE

By following this unique methodology, you will be able to read and write Korean in 40 minutes.

- This is a step-by-step approach. Repetition is encouraged.

- It will allow both new and experienced learners a quick and easy understanding of Korean language structure.

- Reviews at the end of each session will ensure your full comprehension.

- You will have a chance to learn from a list of useful words and expressions.

The words in Korean are made up of combinations of at least one consonant and one vowel.

Let's suppose: The consonants stand for men and the vowels stand for women.

1. A man and a woman get married.

2. The hypothetical family outlook:

   a. The man is responsible for protecting his family: Thus, the husband always comes before in order to protect his household from any danger.

   b. However, this does not mean the husband is dominant over the wife. Rather, it is the wife who exercises influence over the husband.

   c. Thus, positioning of the consonants, either before or over, is dependent upon where the vowels are located. (i.e. if the woman is standing up, her man should likewise be standing up alongside; if she is lying down, then he should be lying over her.)

The Standing Mode

The Lying Mode

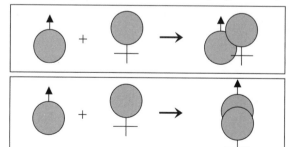

Contents

Korean Characters

CONSONANT GROUP

- 24 characters: 14 consonants and 10 vowels
  (26 in English, 52 in Japanese, and lots in Chinese)

- The 14 consonants are made after the movements of the tongue and the shapes of the mouth.

- The 10 vowels are divided into two modes:
  the standing mode and the lying mode, each of which determines the positions of the consonants.
  (i.e. above the vowel or below it)

= sister

- Each character has its own sound value; and the sounds are made of combinations of the consonants and the vowels.

- Sound syllables are segmentations of a word.
  * One family = One syllable

Yes, you can learn Korean language structure in 40 minutes!

THE 24 CHARACTERS

14 Consonants (Men)

ㄱ ㄴ ㄷ ㄹ ㅁ ㅂ ㅅ ㅈ ㅊ ㅇ ㅋ ㅌ ㅍ ㅎ

10 Vowels (Women)

ㅏ ㅑ ㅓ ㅕ ㅗ ㅛ ㅜ ㅠ ㅡ ㅣ

* A BASIC RULE

"A Man   + A Woman combination" :
  A Consonant + A Vowel combination

$$ ㄱ \quad + \quad ㅏ \quad → \quad 가 $$

a man	+	a woman	→	a couple
a consonant	+	a vowel	→	a word

How many characters are there ?

- The (   ) consonants are made after the movements of Review the tongue and the shapes of the mouth.

- The (   ) vowels are divided into two modes: the standing mode and the lying mode, each of which determines the positions of the consonants.

- The combination rules are very similar to (   ) such as getting married and having children.

- Sound syllables are segmentations of a word.
  * One family = (   ) syllable

KOREAN-ENGLISH SOUND CORRESPONDENCES

14 CONSONANTS		10 VOWELS	
ㄱ	g, k	ㅏ	a
ㄴ	n	ㅑ	ya
ㄷ	d	ㅓ	eo
ㄹ	r, l	ㅕ	yeo
ㅁ	m	ㅗ	o
ㅂ	b, v	ㅛ	yo
ㅅ	s	ㅜ	u
ㅇ	*	ㅠ	yu
ㅈ	j, z	ㅡ	eu
ㅊ	ch	ㅣ	i
ㅋ	k		
ㅌ	t		
ㅍ	p, f		
ㅎ	h		

* "ㅇ" has no sound value in the first position. (e.g. 아)

WORD ORDER

가	[ga]	Garden
나	[na]	Nice
다	[da]	Dawn
라	[la]	Las Vegas
마	[ma]	March
바	[ba]	Barbara
사	[sa]	South
아	[a]	Alphabet
자	[ja]	Jamaica
차	[cha]	China
카	[ka]	Casino
타	[ta]	Time
파	[pa]	Papa
하	[ha]	Harmony

Yes, you can learn Korean language structure in 40 minutes!

Consonants

CONSONANT

The Consonants were designed after **the movements of the tongue and the shapes of the mouth.**

The Five Subgroups

1. Derived from the movements of the tongue (4 characters)

ㄱ g (k)   ㄴ n   ㄷ d   ㄹ r, l

2. Derived from the shapes of the mouth (3 characters)

ㅁ m   ㅂ b, v   ㅍ p

3. Come from the dental sounds (3 characters)

ㅅ s   ㅈ j, z   ㅊ ch

4. Violent sounds (4 characters)

ㅋ k   ㅌ t   ㅍ p   ㅎ h

5. No sound value (in first position)

ㅇ

Yes, you can learn Korean language structure in 40 minutes!

CONSONANTS

(Made after the movements of the tongue)

| | 가 ga | ㄱ |

| | 나 na | ㄴ |

| | 다 da | ㄷ |

| | 라 ra(la) | ㄹ |

* There is no difference in sound between "r" and "l" in Korean.

ㄱ + ㅏ → 가 (g + a → ga)

ㄴ + ㅏ → 나 (n + a → na)

ㄷ + ㅏ → 다 (d + a → da)

가 ga ㄱ

When you make the "가" sound, your tongue curves, from the front ceiling of your mouth, downwards to make the "ㄱ" shape.

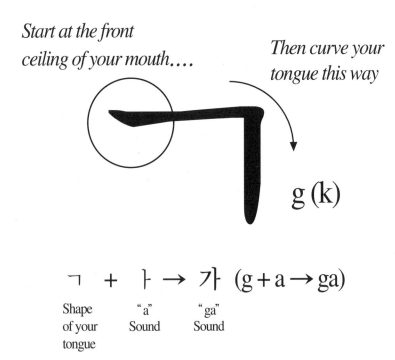

Start at the front ceiling of your mouth....

Then curve your tongue this way

g (k)

ㄱ + ㅏ → 가 (g + a → ga)

| Shape of your tongue | "a" Sound | "ga" Sound |

ㄴ   na   ㄴ

When you make the "ㄴ" sound, your tongue curves, from the front ceiling of your mouth, downwards to make the "ㄴ" shape.

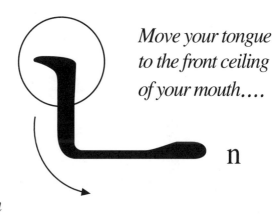

Move your tongue to the front ceiling of your mouth....

n

Then bring it down all the way

ㄴ + ㅏ → ㄴ (n + a → na)

ㄴ	ㅏ	ㄴ
Shape of your tongue	"a" Sound	"na" Sound

다　da　　ㄷ

When you make the "다" sound, your tongue curves, from the center of the front ceiling of your mouth, downwards to make the "ㄷ" shape.

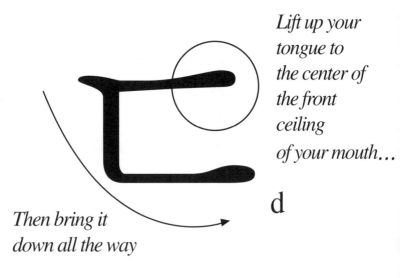

Lift up your tongue to the center of the front ceiling of your mouth...

d

Then bring it down all the way

ㄷ ＋ ㅏ → 다 (d ＋ a → da)

Shape　　　"a"　　　"da"
of your　　Sound　　Sound
tongue

라 ra(la) 근

When you make the "라" sound, your tongue kind of rolls up to make its shape somewhat like the "ㄹ" character.

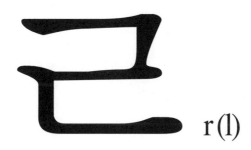

r (l)

ㄹ + ㅏ → 라 (r + a → ra)

Shape   "a"   "ra"   (l + a → la)
of your Sound   Sound
tongue

1. What are the consonants that are made after the movements of your tongue ?

ㄱ ( ) ㄷ ㄹ

2. What are the sound values of these four consonants ?

ㄱ   ㄴ   ㄷ   ㄹ

g   n   d   ( )

CONSONANTS

(Made after the shape of your mouth)

	마 ma	ㅁ
	바 ba(va)	ㅂ
	파 pa	ㅍ

ㅁ + ㅏ → 마 (m + a → ma)

ㅂ + ㅏ → 바 (b + a → ba)

ㅍ + ㅏ → 파 (p + a → pa)

(Made after the shape of your mouth)

마　ma　　ㅁ

The "마" sound can be produced by making your mouth shape like the "ㅁ" character.

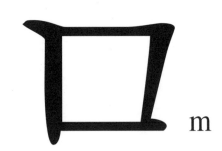

m

ㅁ　+　ㅏ　→　마 (m + a → ma)

Shape of your mouth	"a" Sound	"ma" Sound

CONSONANTS

(Made after the shape of your mouth)

바   ba(va)   ㅂ

The "바" sound can be produced by making your mouth shape like "ㅁ", and then moving your upper lip towards the lower lip.

$$m \qquad\qquad b(v)$$

$$(\Box) \rightarrow ㅂ$$

$$ㅂ \; + \; ㅏ \; \rightarrow \; 바 \quad (b + a \rightarrow ba)$$

Shape of your mouth   " a" Sound   "ba" Sound $(v + a \rightarrow va)$

(Made after the shape of your mouth)

파   pa   프

The "파" sound can be produced by accentuating the "바" sound strongly.

* Please notice how these three sounds are related. Try to pay attention to the related sound among them while going from "마" (ma) to "바" (ba), and likewise from "바" to "파"(pa). Then notice The phonetic connections among them.

$$(\square) \rightarrow (\sqcup) \rightarrow \underline{\underline{\pi}}$$

ma   ba   pa

ㅂ   +   ㅏ   →   파 (p + a → pa)

| Shape of your mouth | "a" Sound | "pa" Sound |

1. What are the consonants that are made after the shapes of your mouth?

ㅁ ( ) ㅍ

2. What are the sound values of the following consonants ?

ㅁ　ㅂ　ㅍ

m　b (v)　( )

CONSONANTS

(Come from the dental sounds)

사　sa　　ㅅ

자　ja(za)　　ㅈ

차　cha　　ㅊ

ㅅ + ㅏ → 사　(s + a → sa)

ㅈ + ㅏ → 자　(j + a → ja)

ㅊ + ㅏ → 차　(ch + a → cha)

Yes, you can learn Korean language structure in 40 minutes!

CONSONANTS

(Come from the dental sounds)

사　sa　　人

When you make the "사" sound, your upper and lower teeth come together to make the shape of the "人" character.

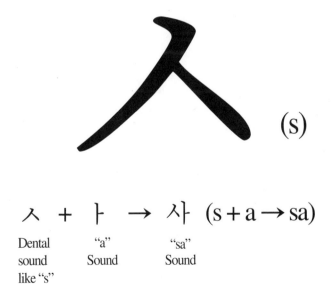

(s)

人　+　ㅏ　→　사　(s + a → sa)

Dental　　"a"　　　"sa"
sound　　Sound　　Sound
like "s"

CONSONANTS

(Come from the dental sounds)

자 ja   ス

When you make the "자" sound, your upper and lower teeth come together to make the shape of "ㅅ". After making the "S" sound, try to pronounce ㅈ by accentuating the sound a little stronger.

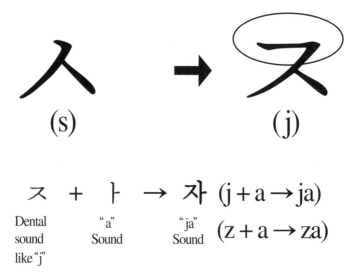

ㅅ → ㅈ

(s)   (j)

ㅈ + ㅏ → 자 $(j + a \rightarrow ja)$

| Dental sound like "j" | "a" Sound | "ja" Sound | $(z + a \rightarrow za)$ |

CONSONANTS

(Come from the dental sounds)

차 ch 　 ㅊ

Likewise, the "차" sound can be produced by accentuating the "자" sound.

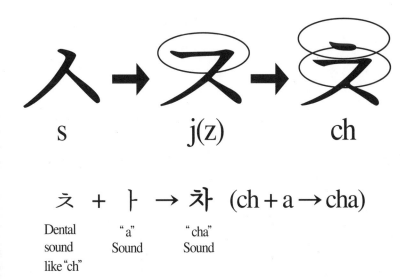

ㅅ → ㅈ → ㅊ

s 　 j(z) 　 ch

ㅊ + ㅏ → 차 (ch + a → cha)

Dental 　 "a" 　 "cha"
sound 　 Sound 　 Sound
like "ch"

1. What are the consonants made after the dental sounds ?

ㅅ ( ) ㅊ

2. What are the sound values of these three consonants ?

ㅅ   ㅈ   ㅊ

s   j(z)   ( )

(Violent Sounds)

가 ga → 카 ka ㅋ

다 da → 타 ta ㅌ

바 ba → 파 pa ㅍ

아 a → 하 ha ㅎ

"아" = "ZERO + ㅏ" combination

"ZERO" : no sound value, silent

Please remember that although vowels (women) can be pronounced without consonant (man), it can not make up a word without the presence of a consonant (man). i.e. ㅏ **(X)** 가**(O)**

CONSONANTS

(Violent Sounds)

가 ga → 카 ka ㅋ

가 + an accent point → 카

카

Yes, you can learn Korean language structure in 40 minutes!

CONSONANTS

(Violent Sounds)

다 da → 타 ta   ㅌ

다 + an accent point → 타

타

CONSONANTS

(Violent Sounds)

바 ba → 파 pa   ㅍ

바 + an accent point → 파

ㅁ	→	ㅂ	→	ㅍ
m		b		p
마		바		파

Yes, you can learn Korean language structure in 40 minutes!

(Violent Sounds)

아 a → 하 ha   ㅎ

아 + an accent point → 하

"ㅏ" can be pronounced by itself, **however** it still needs
"ㅇ" to make up the proper combination.

one consonant + one vowel = one character

The simplest form of a word.

CONSONANTS

No sound value in the consonant (father).
("ng" sound in the second consonant (child) position)

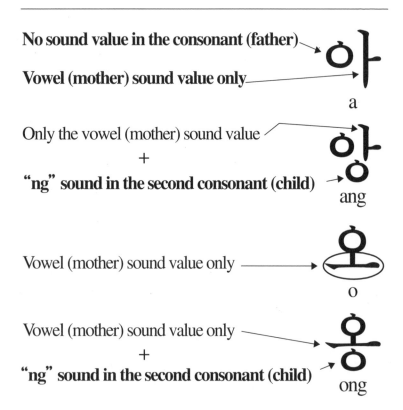

No sound value in the consonant (father)

Vowel (mother) sound value only

a

Only the vowel (mother) sound value
+
"ng" sound in the second consonant (child)

ang

Vowel (mother) sound value only

o

Vowel (mother) sound value only
+
"ng" sound in the second consonant (child)

ong

1. What are the three consonants whose sounds are accentuated?

ㅋ　　(　)　　ㅍ

2. What are the sound values of the three consonants ?

ㅋ　　　　ㅌ　　　　ㅍ
k　　　　t　　　　( )

3. Which consonant has no sound value ?

4. Which consonant has the "ng" sound value in the second consonant (child) position?

Vowels

VOWELS

1. The Standing Mode (5 Vowels)

An arm out to the right   ㅏ

Two arms out to the right   ㅑ

An arm out to the left   ㅓ

Two arms out to the left   ㅕ

No arm out   ㅣ

2. The Lying Mode (5 Vowels)

An arm up   ㅗ

Two arms up   ㅛ

An arm down   ㅜ

Two arms down   ㅠ

No arm up or down   ㅡ

Yes, you can learn Korean language structure in 40 minutes!

1. The Standing Mode (5 Vowels)

An arm out to the right	ㅏ
Two arms out to the right	ㅑ
An arm out to the left	ㅓ
Two arms out to the left	ㅕ
No arm out	ㅣ

Arm

Body

* As the vowel (woman) is standing up, the consonant (man) should be standing up, too. (i.e. "가")

VOWELS

1. The Standing Mode (5 Vowels)

An arm out to the right   ㅏ

ㄱ	+	ㅏ (a)	→	가	ga
ㄴ			→	나	na
ㄷ			→	다	da
ㄹ			→	라	ra
ㅁ			→	마	ma
ㅂ			→	바	ba

Yes, you can learn Korean language structure in 40 minutes!

1. The Standing Mode (5 Vowels)

Two arms out to the right   ㅑ

ㄱ + ㅑ (ya)	→ 가	kya
ㄴ	→ 냐	nya
ㄷ	→ 댜	dya
ㄹ	→ 랴	rya
ㅁ	→ 먀	mya
ㅂ	→ 뱌	bya

1. The Standing Mode (5 Vowels)

An arm out to the left ㅓ

ㅅ	+	ㅓ (eo)	→	서	seo
ㅇ			→	어	eo
ㅈ			→	저	jeo
ㅊ			→	처	cheo
ㅋ			→	커	keo
ㅌ			→	터	teo

VOWELS

1. The Standing Mode (5 Vowels)

Two arms out to the left   ㅕ

ㅅ	+	ㅕ (yeo)	→	셔	syeo
ㅇ			→	여	yeo
ㅈ			→	져	jyeo
ㅊ			→	쳐	chyeo
ㅋ			→	켜	kyeo
ㅌ			→	텨	tyeo

1. The Standing Mode (5 Vowels)

No arm out   ㅣ

ㅅ	+	ㅣ (i)	→	시	si
ㅇ			→	이	i
ㅈ			→	지	ji
ㅊ			→	치	chi
ㅋ			→	키	ki
ㅌ			→	티	ti

1. What vowels are in the standing mode?

( ) ㅑ ( ) ㅕ ㅣ

2. What are the sound values of these five vowels ?

ㅏ ㅑ ㅓ ㅕ ㅣ
( ) ya eo ( ) i

2. The Lying Mode (5 Vowels)

An arm up   ㅗ

Two arms up   ㅛ

An arm down   ㅜ

Two arms down   ㅠ

No arm up or down   —

Arm

Body

* As the vowel (woman) is lying down, the consonant (man) should be lying over the vowel. (e.g. "ㅗ")

2. The Lying Mode (5 Vowels)

An arm up   ㅗ

ㄱ	+	ㅗ (o)	→	고	go
ㄴ			→	노	no
ㄷ			→	도	do
ㄹ			→	로	ro
ㅁ			→	모	mo
ㅂ			→	보	bo

2. The Lying Mode (5 Vowels)

Two arms up ㅛ

ㄱ + ㅛ → 교 gyo
(yo)

ㄴ → 뇨 nyo

ㄷ → 됴 dyo

ㄹ → 료 ryo

ㅁ → 묘 myo

ㅂ → 뵤 byo

2. The Lying Mode (5 Vowels)

An arm down ㅜ

ㄱ + ㅜ → 구 gu

(u)

ㄴ → 누 nu

ㄷ → 두 du

ㄹ → 루 ru

ㅁ → 무 mu

ㅂ → 부 bu

2. The Lying Mode (5 Vowels)

Two arms down   ㅠ

ㅅ	+	ㅠ (yu)	→	슈	syu
ㅇ			→	유	yu
ㅈ			→	쥬	jyu
ㅊ			→	츄	chyu
ㅋ			→	큐	kyu
ㅍ			→	퓨	pyu

2. The Lying Mode (5 Vowels)

No arm up or down   —

ㅅ	+	— (eu)	→	스	seu
ㅇ			→	으	eu
ㅈ			→	즈	jeu
ㅊ			→	츠	cheu
ㅋ			→	크	keu
ㅌ			→	트	teu

1. What vowels are in the lying mode ?

( ) ㅛ ( ) ㅠ ㅡ

2. What are the sound values of these five vowels ?

ㅗ   ㅛ   ㅜ   ㅠ   ㅡ
( )   yo   u   ( )   eu

Words

CONSONANTS & VOWELS

THE COMBINATION MATRIX

	ㄱ	ㄴ	ㄷ	ㄹ	ㅁ	ㅂ	ㅅ
ㅏ	가	나	다	라	마	바	사
ㅑ	갸	냐	댜	랴	먀	뱌	샤
ㅓ	거	너	더	러	머	버	서
ㅕ	겨	녀	뎌	려	며	벼	셔
ㅗ	고	노	도	로	모	보	소
ㅛ	교	뇨	됴	료	묘	뵤	쇼
ㅜ	구	누	두	루	무	부	수
ㅠ	규	뉴	듀	류	뮤	뷰	슈
ㅡ	그	느	드	르	므	브	스
ㅣ	기	니	디	리	미	비	시

Yes, you can learn Korean language structure in 40 minutes!

CONSONANTS & VOWELS

THE COMBINATION MATRIX

	ㅇ	ㅈ	ㅊ	ㅋ	ㅌ	ㅍ	ㅎ
ㅏ	아	자	차	카	타	파	하
ㅑ	야	쟈	챠	캬	탸	퍄	햐
ㅓ	어	저	처	커	터	퍼	허
ㅕ	여	져	쳐	켜	텨	펴	혀
ㅗ	오	조	초	코	토	포	호
ㅛ	요	죠	쵸	쿄	툐	표	효
ㅜ	우	주	추	쿠	투	푸	후
ㅠ	유	쥬	츄	큐	튜	퓨	휴
ㅡ	으	즈	츠	크	트	프	흐
ㅣ	이	지	치	키	티	피	히

THE COMBINATION RULES

- Consonants (fathers) come before and vowels (mothers) come after.
- Fathers always come first.
- Fathers always come before and/or lie over everyone else.
- Occasionally, a man may have two or three wives.
- Occasionally, a man may have two or three wives and a child.
- A woman may likewise have more than one husband and/or child.
- If a woman is standing up, her man should likewise be standing up beside her. If she is lying down, then the man should be lying over her.
- The sound value "o" can be made solely by the vowel "ㅗ". However, as "a woman cannot stand up alone without her man beside her," she still needs her man (a consonant) even though he does not have any sound value.
- Occasionally, a woman may have two husbands and a child.
- Some people may favor sons.
- Some couples may have twins.

THE COMBINATION RULES

1. A man and a woman get married and become a couple:
   One man and one woman make up a couple.

Consonants (fathers) come before and vowels (mothers) come after.

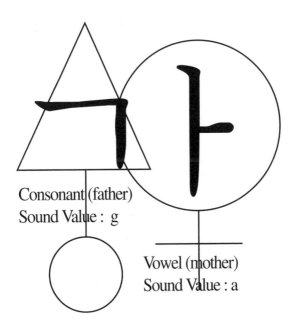

Consonant (father)
Sound Value : g

Vowel (mother)
Sound Value : a

COMBINATION
Sound Value : ga

THE COMBINATION RULES

2-a. The first consonant is the representative of a word.
   (The father is the representative of a family.)

Father always comes before and/or lies over.

correct ➡

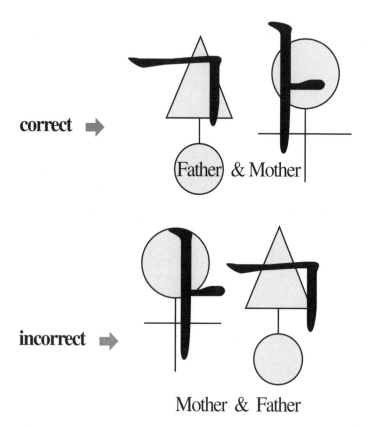

Father & Mother

incorrect ➡

Mother & Father

THE COMBINATION RULES

2-b. Father is the representative of a family.

Thus, Father always comes before and/or over everyone else.

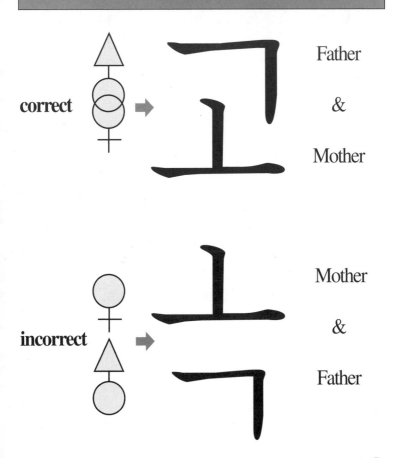

correct → Father & Mother

incorrect → Mother & Father

THE COMBINATION RULES

* Occasionally, a man may have two wives and a woman may likewise have two husbands.

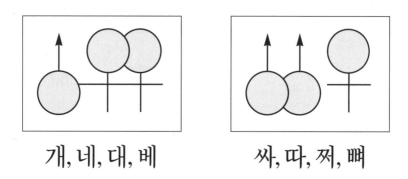

개, 네, 대, 베   싸, 따, 쩌, 뼈

* In all cases...
the consonant (father) should come before.

* The same two consonants may pair up.

correct   ㄲ ㄸ ㅃ ㅆ ㅉ

incorrect   ㅄ   ㄹㄹ   ㅁㄴ

THE COMBINATION RULES

2-c. Occasionally, a man may have two or three wives.

| Man + Women | (1 Man + 2 or 3 Wives) |

ㄱ + ㅏ + ㅣ → 개

g + a + i → gae

ㄷ + ㅗ + ㅏ + ㅣ → 돼

d + o + a + i → dwae

Note

When the ㅣ character is by itself, if can be expressed with the letter "i". However, when it is combined with another vowel (woman), it becomes an "e". This rule applies to the Combination Rules only. [i.e. ㅇㅣ = i, (ㅇㅏ+ㅇㅣ) = a + e]

THE COMBINATION RULES

2-d. Occasionally, a man may have two or three wives and a child.

Father + Mother(s) + Child	(Man + Women + Child)

ㄱ + ㅏ + ㅣ → 개

g + a + i → gae

ㅐ + ㅇ → 갱

+ ng → gaeng

ㄷ + ㅗ + ㅏ + ㅣ → 돼

d + o + a + i → dwae

+ ㄴ → 됀

n dwaen

Note

ㄷ + ㅗ + ㅏ + ㅣ → 돼

d + o + a + i → dwae*

* When the ㅗ and ㅏ characters are combined, it forms a "w" sound in English.

THE COMBINATION RULES

2-e. Occasionally, a woman may have two husbands.

| Men + Woman | (2 Men + 1 Woman) |

ㄷ + ㄷ + ㅏ → 따

d + d + a → tta

ㄱ + ㄱ + ㅏ → 까

g + g + a → kka

THE COMBINATION RULES

3-a. Woman always exercises influences over a man.

3-b. A man's position, either before or over, depends on the woman s.

> (i.e. if she is standing up, her man should likewise be standing up alongside, and if she is lying down, then he should be lying over her.)

If she is standing up, her man should be standing up, too.

Man & Woman

If she is lying down, then the man should be lying over her.

Man
&
Woman

i.e. standing group : 가 갸 거 겨 기
      lying group :   고 교 구 규 그

THE COMBINATION RULES

3-c. A woman may exercise influence over her man, yet she cannot stand up alone without her man alongside.

> The sound value "o" can be made solely by the vowel "ㅗ" . However, as "a waman cannot stand up alone without her man alongside, she still needs her man (a consonant), though he has no sound value.

So, we use ZERO, "O" for this.

아   ➡   ZERO + a → a

야   ➡   ZERO + ya → ya

오   ➡   ZERO + o → o

요   ➡   ZERO + yo → yo

■ Characters that start with "O" (ZERO) have no sound value as consonants. They only have vowel sounds.

THE COMBINATION RULES

3-d. Occasionally, a woman may has two husbands and a child.

Father + Mother(s) + Child

(2 Men + 1 Woman + 1 Child)

ㄷ + ㄷ + ㅏ → 따

d + d + a → tta

+ ㄹ → 딸

l　　　　ttal

ㄱ + ㄱ + ㅏ → 까

g + g + a → kka

+ ㅁ → 깜

m　　　　kkam

Yes, you can learn Korean language structure in 40 minutes!

THE COMBINATION RULES

* Some couples have two children.

a. Sometimes a couple has twins (dual second consonants).

b. Children (dual second consonants) are never to come before as long as their parents are alive.

The father (consonant) comes before,
the mother (vowel) after
the children (dual second consonants) follow.

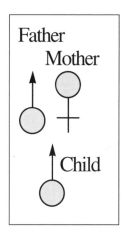

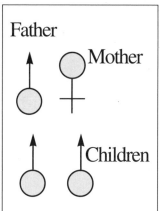

박, 선, 당   닭, 밝, 삶   손, 봉, 국

THE COMBINATION RULES

4-a. Boys are "preferred" to girls.

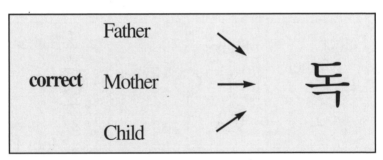

Parents   ㅂ + ㅏ

Child   + ㅁ → 밤

■ Father comes before, Mother after. The child follows.

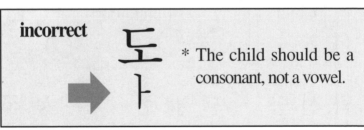

correct

Father

Mother → 독

Child

incorrect

도
ㅏ

* The child should be a consonant, not a vowel.

THE COMBINATION RULES

4-b. Some families have twins.

Parents
ㄷ + ㅏ

Twins (same characters)
+ ㄲ → 닦

(d + a + k → dak)

Parents
ㄷ + ㅏ

Two children
(different characters)
+ ㄹㄱ → 닭

(d + a + k → dak)

* No more than two children are necessary for the purpose of this study.

Note

In instances where there are double consonants, (e.g. ㅆ) or two separate consonants (e.g. ㄹㄱ), there are two English letters corresponding to the same number of Korean characters, according to this particular romanization system. It should be noted, however, that only one letter is pronounced. So, as in the case of 닭, although it is written "dakk" in English, it is simply pronounced "dak."

Sound Syllables & Word Segments

SOUND SYLLABLES & WORD SEGMENTS

* One family, one syllable principle

호 텔
HO TEL

➡

ㅎ + ㅗ	ㅌ + ㅓ + ㅣ + ㄹ

(HOTEL) ⬅ HO + TEL
(Two Syllables)

스미스
SMITH

➡

ㅅ + ㅡ	ㅁ + ㅣ	ㅅ + ㅡ
SEU +	MI +	SEU

존슨
JOHNSON

➡

ㅈ + ㅗ + ㄴ	ㅅ + ㅡ + ㄴ
JON +	SEUN

Yes, you can learn Korean language structure in 40 minutes!

Sound Syllables & Word Segments

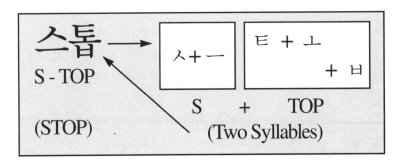

스톱 ⟶

스 + ─

ㅌ + ㅗ
+ ㅂ

S - TOP

S + TOP

(STOP)

(Two Syllables)

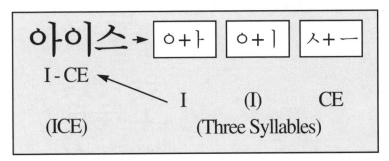

아이스 ⟶

ㅇ + ㅏ

ㅇ + ㅣ

스 + ─

I - CE ⟵

I   (I)   CE

(ICE)

(Three Syllables)

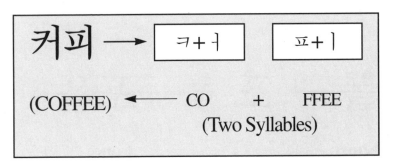

커피 ⟶

ㅋ + ㅓ

ㅍ + ㅣ

(COFFEE) ⟵ CO + FFEE

(Two Syllables)

* One couple (family) has one syllable.

Sound syllables are segments of a word.
In this case, you can pronounce one English word in two different ways.

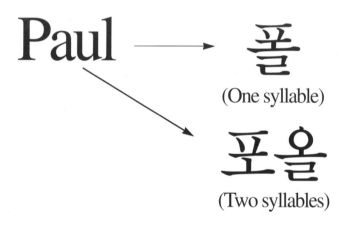

Paul ⟶ 폴
(One syllable)

포올
(Two syllables)

폴 → 포-ㄹ →포올

**Short
Pronunciation**

**Long
Pronunciation**

Vocabulary: a selected list

NUMBERING SYSTEM

Numbers	Pure Korean Numbers		Chinses Derived Numbers	
1	하나	hana	일	il
2	둘	dul	이	i
3	셋	set	삼	sam
4	넷	net	사	sa
5	다섯	daseot	오	o
6	여섯	yeoseot	육	yuk
7	일곱	ilgop	칠	chil

Yes, you can learn Korean language structure in 40 minutes!

NUMBERING SYSTEM

Numbers	Pure Korean Numbers		Chinses Derived Numbers	
8	여덟	yeodeol	팔	pal
9	아홉	ahop	구	gu
10	열	yeol	십	sip
11	열하나	yeol-hana	십일	sip-il
12	열둘	yeol-dul	십이	sip-i
13	열셋	yeol-set	십삼	sip-sam
20	스물	seumul	이십	i-sip

Numbers	Pure Korean Numbers		Chinses Derived Numbers	
21	스물 하나	seumul-hana	이십 일	i-sip-il
22	스물 둘	seumul-dul	이십 이	i-sip-i
30	서른	seoreun	이십 삼	i-sip-sam
40	마흔	maheun	사십	sa-sip
50	쉰	swim	오십	o-sip
60	예순	yesun	육십	yuk-sip
70	이른	ilheun	칠십	chil-sip

NUMBERING SYSTEM

Numbers	Pure Korean Numbers		Chinses Derived Numbers	
80	여든	yeodeun	팔십	pal-sip
90	아흔	aheun	구십	gu-sip
100	백	baek	백	baek
1,000	천	cheon	천	cheon
10,000	만	man	만	man
100,000	십만	sip-man	십만	sip-man
1,000,000	백만	baek-man	백만	baek-man

CURRENCY UNIT

Basic unit : won (원)

Coins

10 won
50 won
100 won
500 won

Bills

1,000 won
5,000 won
10,000 won

Yes, you can learn Korean language structure in 40 minutes!

NUMERIC COUNTING SYSTEM

1	10	100	1000	10,000
일	십	백	천	만
il	sip	baek	cheon	man

100,000	1,000,000	10,000,000
십만	백만	천만
sip-man	baek-man	cheon-man

100,000,000	1,000,000,000
일억	십억
il-eok	sip-eok

10,000,000,000	100,000,000,000
백억	천억
baek-eok	cheon-eok

1,000,000,000,000
일조
il-jo

10,000,000,000,000
십조
sip-jo

KOREAN NAMES

■ To address someone with his or her full name, the family name comes first, then the first name.

* The three most common family names are Kim, Lee and Park.

* Usually a name has three syllables:　김　영　복
  • The first syllable is the family name.
  • The next two syllables that follow are the given name.

* Some names have only two syllables:　이　준
  • The family name comes first
  • The given name follows.

* Few names have four syllables:　황보　지은
  • The first two syllables are the family name.
  • The next two syllables that follow are the given name.

■ Addressing someone with their family name is considered much more polite.

■ Except for children and those who are younger than you, people are not to be addressed with their given names only, but rather with their full names or titles.

■ Names entail a special meaning to Koreans thus, people dignify others' names, and expect the same from others in return.

SAMPLE NAMES

| Three syllables | 김 | 대　　중 |
| | Family Name | Given Name |

| Three syllables | 박 | 정　　희 |
| | Family Name | Given Name |

| Two syllables | 김 | 영 |
| | Family Name | Given Name |

| Four syllables | 선 우 | 정　　선 |
| | Family Name | Given Name |

SELECTED NAMES IN KOREAN

Paul	폴
Jane	제인
Robert	로버트
Diana	다이아나
Tom	톰
Juliet	줄리엣
Peter	피터
Anna	애나
David	데이빗
Johan	요한
Julia	줄리아
Margaret	마가렛
Maria	마리아

Yes, you can learn Korean language structure in 40 minutes!

THE KOREAN DYNASTIES

조선
(CHOSUN)

Between the 14th - 20th centuries
(1392-1910)
The last dynasty of Korea.
The name means
"MORNING CALM".

고려
(KOREA)

Between the 10th - 14th centuries.
The name means
"HIGH & BEAUTIFUL".

- During its time, Korea had made its initial introduction to Europe, and since then the name "Korea" has become official in the international system.

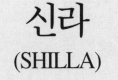

신라
(SHILLA)

Between 57 B.C. - 935 A.D.
The kingdom of Shilla had lasted for almost 1000 years.

* It was the first unified kingdom on the Korean peninsula.
- Gyeongju, the capital at the time, is now very popular among tourists for its profound antiquities.

THE ADDRESS ORDER

Country	대한민국*
Province (or the Special City)	서울특별시
City	- - -
District	용산구
Street	한강로 2가
Lot	191번지
Building and floor	국제빌딩 19 층
Company name	삼 일 C & L
Title and name	이사 이동구

Country	대한민국
Province	경상남도
City	진해시
Village	여좌동
House	63번지
Name	홍길동

It goes from the largest administrative unit to smaller units, and then to the party s name.

* 대한민국 : The Republic of Korea

USEFUL WORDS

아버지	Father
어머니	Mother
할아버지	Grandfather
할머니	Grandmother
형님 or 오빠	Elder brother
남동생	Younger brother
여동생	Younger sister
회사	Company
사장	President
임원	Executive
사원	Employee
사규	Regulation
본사	Headquarters
지사	Branch office

Around the World

미국	USA
영국	UK
프랑스	France
독일	Germany
러시아	Russia
일본	Japan
뉴욕	New York
런던	London
파리	Paris
베를린	Berlin
모스크바	Moscow
토쿄	Tokyo

Yes, you can learn Korean language structure in 40 minutes!

KOREAN CUISINE

The three main dishes that make up a meal:

• **밥:** Has three meanings
1. The main dish
2. Rice
3. The meal itself (i.e. breakfast, lunch, dinner)

• **국:** Soup

• **반찬:** Side dishes

  * **김치 :** Kimchi (pickled vegetables)

수저 : the spoons and the chopsticks

* A common meal would include a bowl of white rice, a few small side dishes and a bowl of soup.

* Kimchi is the most popular side dish.

* Some of the most popular spices include red peppers, sesame oil, soy souse and garlic.

* The Koreans, unlike the Japanese or the Chinese, eat steamed (sticky) rice and soup with their spoons.

서울 **SEOUL — The Capital**
• Populated with approximately 12 million people (a quarter of the entire population of South Korea).

부산 **BUSAN**
• Located in the southeast--the largest harbor city.

대구 **DAEGU**
• Located north of Busan--the third largest city in Korea.

대전, 광주, 경주
Daejeon, Gwangju, Gyeongju

• The National Flag

Taegeukgi

• The National Flower

무궁화

The Rose of
Sharon

• The National Bird

까치

Magpie

Korea is also known as

The Land of Morning Calm (조선)

ARMY RANKS

General	대 장
Lieutenant General	중 장
Major General	소 장
Brigadier General	준 장
Colonel	대 령
Lieutenant Colonel	중 령
Major	소 령
Captain	대 위
1st Lieutenant	중 위
2nd Lieutenant	소 위
Warrant Officer	준 위
Master Sergeant	상 사
Sergeant 1st Class	중 사
Step Sergeant	하 사
Sergeant	병 장
Corporal	상 병
Private First Class	일등병
Private	이등병

Yes, you can learn Korean language structure in 40 minutes!

SCHOOL SYSTEMS

초등　　학교 chodeung hakgyo	Elementary School
중등　　학교 jungdeung hakgyo	Middle School
고등　　학교 godeung hakgyo	High School
대 학교 dae hakgyo	University or College

"학교"	means	School
"초등"	means	Primary grades
"중등"	means	Middle grades
"고등"	means	High grades
"대"	means	Great

THE KOREAN ZODIAC SYSTEM

띠		Year of Birth		
쥐	Mouse	'60	'48	'36
소	Ox (Cow)	'61	'49	'37
호랑이	Tiger	'62	'50	'38
토끼띠	Rabbit	'63	'51	'39
용	Dragon	'64	'52	'40
뱀	Snake	'65	'53	'41
말	Horse	'66	'54	'42
양	Sheep	'67	'55	'43
원숭이	Monkey	'68	'56	'44
닭	Cock	'69	'57	'45
개	Dog	'70	'58	'46
돼지	Pig	'71	'59	'47

* Each year has it's own symbol of animal symbol.
  e.g. 1960 is the year of the Mouse.

Yes, you can learn Korean language structure in 40 minutes!

MODES OF TRANSPORTATION

버스	Bus
택시	Taxi
자동차	Automobile
기차	Train
지하철	Subway
오토바이	Motorcycle
자전거	Bicycle
비행기	Airplane
배	Ship / Boat
표	Ticket
운임	Fare / Charge

DRINKS

1. Soft Drinks (Soda) 탄산음료

Coke	콜라 * 'Coke' is generally called 'Cola' in Korea.
7UP / Sprite	사이다
Orange Juice	오렌지주스
Water	물
Mineral Spring Water	광천수

2. Liquors 술

Beer	맥주
Scotch	스카치
Brandy	브랜디
Sake	정종 or 사케
Rum	럼
White Wine	흰 포도주
Red Wine	붉은 포도주
Soju (distilled liquor)	소주

Yes, you can learn Korean language structure in 40 minutes!

UTICITIES

1. Electric power unit

Voltage   :   AC 220 V at 60 Hz
Outlet   :   Plugs with round tips

(May work with in some European models but not in American or Japanese ones.)

2. Telephone numbers

Country code   :   82
Area codes (omit 0's when dialing overseas)
서울 Seoul   :   02
부산 Busan   :   051
대전 Daejun   :   052
대구 Daegu   :   053

Digit numbers : Mostly three and four, or four and four
digits (e.g. 536-1234)

DIRECTIONS

Here	여기	Yeogi
There	저기	Jeogi
Where	어디	Eodi
Faraway	멀리	Meolli
Near	가까이	Gakkai
Right Side	오른쪽	Oreunjjok
Left Side	왼쪽	Oenjjok
Middle	가운데	Gaunde

Yes, you can learn Korean language structure in 40 minutes!

Formulating
Sentences

THE GROUND RULES OF WORD ORDER

English : I am going to school.

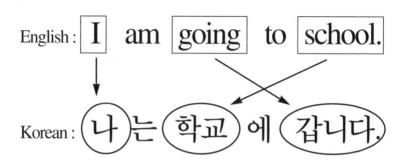

Korean : 나는 학교 에 갑니다.

Simplified (colloquial) : 학교 에 갑니다
(school, to, going)

You are reading a book.

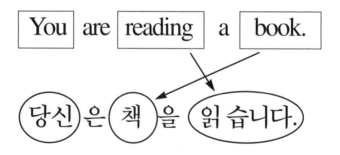

당신은 책을 읽습니다.

Simplified (colloquial) : 책 을 읽습니다
(book, reading)

AFFIRMATIVE VS. INTERROGATIVE

A : 학교   에   갑니**다**.
School   to   Going .

I : 학교   에   갑니**까** ?
School   to   Going ?

A : 책   을   읽습니**다**.
Book   Reading .

I : 책   을   읽습니**까** ?
Book   Reading ?

* Interrogatives always have rising intonation.

AFFIRMATIVE VS. INTERROGATIVE

A: 집 에 갑니**다**.
Home to Going .

I: 집 에 갑니**까**?
Home to Going ?

A: 친구 를 만납니**다**.
Friend Seeing .

I: 친구 를 만납니**까**?
Friend Seeing ?

* Interrogatives always have rising intonation.

 Yes, you can learn Korean language structure in 40 minutes!

AFFIRMATIVE VS. INTERROGATIVE

여기 책 이 있습니**다**.
Here Book There is .

여기 책 이 있습니**까**?
Here Book Is there ?

저기 책 이 있습니**다**.
There Book There is .

저기 책 이 있습니**까**?
There Book Is there ?

여기   책 이   없습니**다**.

Here   Book   There is no.

여기   책 이   없습니**까**?

Here   Book   Is there no ?

저기   책 이   없습니**다**.

There   Book   There is no.

저기   책 이   없습니**까**?

There   Book   Is there no ?

여기 큰 책 이 있습니다.
Here   BIG   Book   There is .

여기 큰 책 이 있습니까 ?
Here   BIG   Book   Is there ?

저기 큰 책 이 있습니다.
There   BIG   Book   There is .

저기 큰 책 이 있습니까 ?
There   BIG   Book   Is there ?

여기 작은 책이 있습니다.

Here **SMALL** Book There is.

여기 작은 책이 있습니까 ?

Here **SMALL** Book Is there ?

저기 작은 책이 있습니다.

There **SMALL** Book There is.

저기 작은 책이 있습니까 ?

There **SMALL** Book Is there ?

SHOPPING

This	이것	Igeot
That	저것	Jeogeot
How much	얼마	Eolma
The bigger one	큰 것	Keun geot
The smaller one	작은 것	Jageun geot

How much is this ?

이것 은	얼마	입니까 ?
this	How much	is ?
Igeoteun	**eolma**	imni**kka** ?

* 입니 **까** ? : Interrogative

SHOPPING

Q : How much is this ?

이것은 **얼마** 입니까 ?

A : That is 100 dollars.

그것은 **백 달러** 입니다.

It's too expensive.

너무 비쌉니다.

Can you offer me a little cheaper one?

조금 **싼** 것을 주시겠습니까?

MAKING IT POLITE / REFINED

To school,   **Go (-ing)** / **Go (-ing) ?**

학교 에,   갑니다   / 갑니까 ?

        간다   / 가니 ?

        가십니다 / 가십니까 ?

갑니다 : Formal
(갑니까 ?) Used with strangers

간다 : Informal or casual
(가니 ?) Used with close friends

가십니다 : Honorific
(가십니까 ?) Used with people of authority
and with much older people
(e.g. parents, teachers, superiors, etc.)

안녕 하십니까 ?

Annyeong   ha-sip-ni-kka ?

Meaning : Are you all right? Are you happy and healthy ?

Use:

Greetings
- Good morning
- Good afternoon
- How are you?
- Hello (Hi)

"안녕" is the key word: "Happy and Healthy"

(ANNYEONG)

안녕히 가십시오.

Annyeong-hi   ga-sip-si-o.

Meaning : Please have a safe and peaceful journey.

Use: **Good-byes**

 Yes, you can learn Korean language structure in 40 minutes!

Appendix

(FORMULAS)

1. 14 consonants &
   10 vowels, each with
   their own sound values-
   Let say,
   Consonants stand for Men and
   Vowels stands for women.

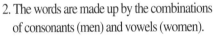

ㄱ	g (k)	ㅏ	a
ㄴ	n	ㅑ	ya
ㄷ	d	ㅓ	eo
ㄹ	r, l	ㅕ	yeo
ㅁ	m	ㅗ	o
ㅂ	b, v	ㅛ	yo
ㅅ	s	ㅜ	u
ㅇ	o(ZERO)*	ㅠ	yu
ㅈ	j, z	ㅡ	eu
ㅊ	ch	ㅣ	i
ㅋ	k		
ㅌ	t		
ㅍ	p		
ㅎ	h		

2. The words are made up by the combinations
   of consonants (men) and vowels (women).

   2-1 A man and a woman get married -> a FAMILY

   2-2 Man may have 2 or 3 wives and

   2-3 Woman may likewise have 2 husbands.

   2-4 Or any given two men may have two wives.

   2-5 Man (consonant) always comes before and/or
       lies over everyone else.

   2-5-1 Man (consonant) should come before his wife
         when she is standing up.

   2-5-2 Man (consonant) should be lying over his
         wife when she is lying down.

3. Some people may favor sons

   3-1 Son always follows his parents.

   3-1-1 Father (Man) comes before,
         Mother (woman) after. The then son follows.

   3-1-2 Some families may have 2 sons.

 or